The

SECRET to

REAL ESTATE

The Secret to Real Estate, LLC

www.TheSecretToRealEstate.com

The SECRET to REAL ESTATE

Leveraging Government Plans and Projects

Adam R. Katz, M.S.
The Secret to Real Estate, LLC

www.TheSecretToRealEstate.com

Edited by Hayley Worthman, M.A. & Ula Manzo, Ph.D, Professor Emeritus, California State University, Fullerton

Cover Photo by Susan Manzur – SusanManzur.com

Cover Designed by Moka Graphics – ThinkMoka.com

Print Typesetting by Grzegorz Laszczyk – GrzegorzLaszczyk.pl

ISBN-13: 978-0692591376
ISBN-10: 0692591370
Besiyata Dishmaya Publications
The Secret to Real Estate, LLC
www.TheSecretToRealEstate.com
Adam@thesecrettorealestate.com
Brooklyn, New York

To my wife, the Bubbie, my parents, my siblings, my uncles, my aunts, my cousins, my new California family, and those friends that have become family. To the whole Mishpacha.

About the Author

Adam R. Katz, M.S., is the founder and owner of *The Secret to Real Estate, LLC*, a real estate coaching and advising firm in New York City. Through his company, he has coached investors, agents, and others from across the United States on strategies for making more money in their residential real estate ventures. Adam has earned a Masters degree in Urban and Regional Policy with a focus on Economic Development from Northeastern University. Some of his experience includes working in a think tank advising mayors and town managers how to strategically grow their municipalities, assisting in the revitalization of the famous Coney Island, and conducting extensive academic research on U.S. property values.

Contents

Foreword

It was a mere twenty six hundred years ago, in Ancient Greece, when the idea of a "downtown" first came into existence. Known as "the agora," meaning "open-air gathering place," it was the political and commercial center, the heart, of city-states such as Athens. For as long as I can remember, I have been enamored with downtowns and municipalities. Even after exploring countless cities throughout the world, from Cairo to Tokyo to Paris to Jerusalem, earning a Master's Degree in Urban and Regional Policy, and consulting for state, city, and town leaders, the mystique and grandeur of municipalities still puts me in a state of awe each time I step out of my Brooklyn home or explore a new part of the world.

Towns, cities, and downtowns each have their own unique character and personality. They can be busy and loud or calm and quiet. Some are hubs of technology, art, education, or medicine. Others are centers of shopping, entertainment, or tourism, and yet others are home to vast parks, outdoor activities, and open spaces. Each has its own set of specialties and thus attracts relevant residents and visitors.

Every municipality has its own powerful energy and takes on a life of its own. That life needs to be supported, however. Where does this support come from? From *economic development,* my area of expertise. I have dedicated my career and education to learning and practicing the art and science of economic development – to building and growing towns, cities, and downtowns.

How does economic development come into play in terms of property values? It's simple really. When a municipality practices particular, solid economic development principles that result in community growth, property values generally increase. Since economic development is the key to growth, it is also the key to property values. That is the point of this book: to give you the tools to understand the secrets of economic development so you can better predict and capitalize on the future.

1. Introduction

"The strategic use of knowledge is the secret to success."

—Adam R. Katz, M.S.

Background

I am the Founder and Owner of *The Secret to Real Estate, LLC,* a real estate coaching and advising firm located in New York City. In my firm, I train agents, brokers, investors, developers, and homebuyers to view real estate from a new perspective. Through one-on-one coaching, seminars, webinars, online courses, workshops, and other services, I give my clients the tools they need to help them better predict future residential property value increases so that they can make more money. That is the lens through which I wrote this book.

I have cultivated my real estate and economic development skills and knowledge through:

- Advising mayors, town managers, and planners throughout New England how to write Economic Development Strategies and Master Plans to grow their towns and cities – a service that has impacted over 300,000 people.
- Recommending strategies to the Massachusetts Office of Housing and Economic Development to meet the goal of the Governor to build more multi-family housing.
- Earning a Master's Degree in Urban and Regional Policy with a focus on Economic Development from Northeastern University.
- Coaching real estate professionals from throughout the country, from New York City to Los Angeles to Boston.
- Working to revitalize the famous Coney Island in New York City.
- Extensively reviewing over 650 academic studies and reports of impacts on United States property values.
- Investing in residential property in Massachusetts.
- Working at the Dukakis Center for Urban and Regional Policy Think [and Do] Tank at Northeastern University.

This book will distill much of my knowledge, experience, and research on urban and suburban property values into a simple, educational guide that you will be able to use immediately in your real estate ventures.

How this Book Can Help You

Through reading and following the advice and instructions in this book, you will be able to quickly discover whether there is relevant, planned growth in your urban and suburban target areas. This knowledge, and its application, will help you make a prediction about property values, and you will therefore be able to purchase property or land *before* values increase.

This book is for real estate agents, brokers, investors, developers, and homebuyers who are looking to up their game and make more money selling and buying residential homes and condominiums. You will learn to think in a new way: about the future and about "what can be," which is the way *mayors* think.

If you are a real estate agent or broker, you will learn to:

- Gain a competitive edge over the other two million real estate licensees in the U.S.
- Farm neighborhoods and focus your efforts where you expect property values to increase . . . and in areas no one else knows.
- Sell more property.

- Close deals quicker by giving buyers a sense of urgency when you inform them of your expectations of increased property values.
- Turn more leads into buyers.
- Turn single buyers into repeat buyers.
- Attract more referrals based on your "secret" knowledge.
- Make fewer cold calls since leads will come to you.
- Analyze neighborhoods on a new level.
- Get higher sales prices and satisfy your sellers more.
- Reduce advertising costs and time since leads will come to you.
- Satisfy your buyers more when their property values increase.

If you are an investor or developer, you will learn to:
- Target neighborhoods and municipalities
- Invest only in areas with anticipated growth.
- Raise more money from other investors.
- Attract more investors.
- Improve the odds of higher ROIs (Returns On Investment).
- Help build property value safety cushions into your investments as a hedge against recessions and inflation.
- Help your developments fit in better with the town and its future plans, improving your odds of success.

- Know when it's time to buy, before property values rise.

If you are a homebuyer, you will learn to:
- Feel comfortable knowing that the biggest purchase you will ever make is a smarter investment.
- Gain peace of mind knowing that your new home is located in an area with anticipated growth.
- Help build a property value safety cushion into your investment as a hedge against recessions and inflation.
- Know when it's time to buy, before property values rise.

It's all about Property Value

Property value. Property value. Property value. That's what your buyers want. That's what you want as an investor. That's what you want as a homeowner. One of the most important questions is, "will the property value increase?" What if you could predict changes in property values before they occurred? How much more money would you make? I am going to give you the tools to help you make these predictions.

Let me explain using a movie analogy. Have you ever seen the 2011 baseball movie, "Moneyball" about the Oakland A's? The premise is that the General Manager, Billy Beane (Brad Pitt), and the Assistant General Manager, Peter Brand (Jonah Hill), build a solid baseball team using a new analytical approach. This approach adds a whole new layer of understanding of the players and the game, and also adds some predictability regarding the players' performance. This is what my book can do for you in your residential real estate activities. You will "up your game," adding this new layer of analysis and predictability.

With regard to anticipated property value increases, every real estate professional's "game" is about the same. There are certain factors that everybody knows affect property values, such as good schools, beautiful homes, wealthy demographics, parks, fancy developments, etc. This book is not really about these imperative elements, although several of those factors are included. This book is about plans and trends that change continuously and result from active efforts or even sprout up organically. The methods included in this book will help you identify these plans and trends; these methods are the *secrets* that will help you predict future property value increases. After learning this information, you will no longer be a simple real estate professional or homebuyer, but a savvy one, armed with skills and knowledge that will set you apart from the competition.

Remember, the strategic use of knowledge is the secret to success.

How to Use this Book

I have designed the layout of this book in an easily digestible way. Each chapter contains a different economic development concept, and within each chapter are subtitles to help you understand, identify, and predict the future.

The layout of each chapter is as follows:

Chapter Title: Economic Development Concept
      Subtitle: What Is It?
      Subtitle: Why Is It Important?
      Subtitle: How To Think About It?
      Subtitle: Where To Find [the information]?
      Subtitle: Example/s
      Subtitle: How To Present It [to buyers and
              investors]?

Each economic development concept is a good **indicator** of potential growth in a community: an indicator of a stronger likelihood that the community or neighborhood would be a lucrative investment.

No one municipality, which I define as any town or city, will have all the concepts discussed in this book. Therefore, in addition to looking for these concepts in your target municipality, look in your surrounding region. Perhaps you will discover that a small town ten miles from yours has the potential for major growth.

So, you will then capitalize and start to tap into that housing market by selling or investing in homes there.

2. To Keep in Mind

No Guarantees
With complex municipal operations, touchy political territory, community opposition, planning board rejections, and countless other factors affecting plans and projects, there are no guarantees in real estate. However, this book will help serve as a guide for you to know how to choose wiser investments and recommend properties so you can make more money.

Be Smart
Always consider more than one factor when making real estate decisions. Economic development does not exist in a vacuum, and the outcomes of initiatives are affected by many factors. Certain factors, such as criminal activity, may greatly weaken or eliminate the positive effect of an economic development initiative. Also, always compare current property values to historic values to ensure that the increases have not already occurred.

Solid Economic Development Principles

It is very important that the project, strategy, or development that a municipality is undertaking is based upon solid economic development principles and is of a high caliber. Those types of projects are the ones that are most likely to succeed and increase property values.

It's Not a 'Get-Rich-Quick' Scheme

This book is not about short-term investments. It is not a get-rich-quick scheme. The advice contained in this book can help guide your real estate ventures so you can better choose properties that are more likely to increase in property values. These values take time to change, especially when you are basing your decision on potential future outcomes.

Urban vs. Suburban

Unless I have specifically stated that a particular project or initiative affects only an urban or suburban area, you can safely assume that the project or initiative will affect both types of areas.

3. Research

Research Skills

Research is a central skill you will develop through reading and practicing the tools in this book. In order to analyze neighborhoods, towns, and cities, you will need to first find the information to analyze. You will learn to quickly dig deep and sift through planning documents, municipal websites, Google, and more. You will also become comfortable with making telephone calls to municipal government offices to learn information, and this will be a key source of your knowledge.

Google Research Secret

If it has not already happened, Google will now be your best friend. There is a search secret to Google that will help you quickly find much of the information you will need (although calling the municipality directly is always the best source of up-to-date information). You will want to use this secret for every chapter and for all future research to save you tremendous amounts of time.

To utilize this Google search secret in the most advantageous way, follow these instructions:

1. Find the website for your target municipality. For example, let's use the city of Quincy, Massachusetts, which is where I was born. The website is www.quincyma.gov.

2. Go to Google.com

3. Type the following italicized text in your browser: *site:www.quincyma.gov*, but do not hit the search button yet.

4. Let's say you want to now search for economic development activities in Quincy. To do so, add the following italicized text, *economic development*, immediately after what you have already typed in the search box. So it will appear in the search box as: *site:www.quincyma.gov economic development*.

5. Hit the search button now. Instead of Google now searching all sites on the internet for your text, it will search only Quincy's municipal website for the phrase "economic development."

The first site to pop up is Quincy's economic development page, the second is the city's Planning and Community Development Department page, and the third is the city's Economic Development Report. These three sources of information are key to understanding the economic development climate and undertakings in Quincy.

You can use this secret to search any municipal website for any topic or concept, and the search results will always be useful. For proof, use this secret to browse your target municipality for "economic development" and see what the Google results yield. You will learn exactly what to look for throughout the following chapters in this book.

4. Free Resources, Linked-In Group, and Exclusive Discounts

The field of economic development and real estate is constantly evolving, so my goal for you is to always maintain a competitive edge. Therefore, as the founder and owner of *The Secret to Real Estate, LLC*, I will continually create resources and conduct research to help you sustain, grow, and sharpen that edge.

The first free resource that you are invited to utilize is my networking group on Linked-In called, "The Secret to Real Estate Networking Group." By joining, you will expand your professional network, have access to powerful real estate players, learn about my webinars and online courses, discover new deals, share ideas, and see my handpicked real estate articles. The second free resource is a special section of my website *only* for my book readers. By subscribing to emails from me, I will personally send you invitations to webinars and online courses, share new discoveries about property values, trends, and real estate, and offer *exclusive* Book Reader discounts. To subscribe, visit:

www.TheSecretToRealEstate.com/BookSecrets.html

5. Economic Development Strategies and Master Plans

What Are They?

Economic Development Strategies and Master Plans can be goldmines of information for you regarding your target community. These documents outline the goals of a municipality and the initiatives it plans to undertake to achieve the goals. They are essentially roadmaps a municipality plans to follow, and these specified goals and undertakings are key to understanding the direction and growth of a particular community. Therefore, these documents are the first places you should look to get an overall understanding of any area. The information contained within them is what will help you form a prediction about future property values.

An Economic Development Strategy, which may be a standalone document or a section within a Master Plan, may focus on only certain initiatives, typically considered "economic development," within a municipality. However, the term "economic development" is vague, and is not limited to new businesses, job creation, and redevelopment. *Everything* is economic development, from new sewer infrastructure to land rezoning to tree plantings. A Master Plan is more likely to focus on all initiatives, and is therefore just a more comprehensive version of an economic development strategy. If a municipality has both an Economic Development Strategy and Master Plan, you will want to review both.

Why Are They Important?

These documents are your guide to a municipality. What are its leaders planning? What may the future hold for that location? Knowing what is being planned gives you a glimpse into the future, which gives you a sense of how property values may change.

How To Think About Them?

When reviewing the Economic Development Strategies and Master Plans, search for actual, concrete plans, not what the municipality would "like to do" or "should do." Do not base any of your determinations on "Needs Assessments." You will want to make sure your determination is based upon concrete plans or activities that have recently commenced. You will also want to find answers to the following questions: Has the planning board approved the project? Has the project commenced? How close to completion is the undertaking? What is the timeline? Perhaps a particular project is due to begin in a month – if that is the case, that means that now could quite possibly be a wise time to buy.

You will want to skim these documents for the concepts outlined in this book. You must remember, though, that just because a topic or initiative is not labeled "Economic Development" that does not mean it is *not* economic development. Therefore, if you are looking in a Master Plan, review the whole document, not just the Economic Development section.

While skimming the documents, keep the big picture questions in mind. Which locations or neighborhoods within the municipality are the leadership focusing on? Where is it investing major resources and funds? Which neighborhoods are mentioned repeatedly? Oftentimes, municipalities dedicate resources to revitalizing specific districts, such as downtown areas or certain residential or commercial neighborhoods. Keep in mind that if the municipality plans to revitalize its northeastern corner, property values on the southwestern corner may not necessarily increase at all as a result of the revitalization. Location and proximity are key factors to take into consideration.

Although Economic Development Strategies and Master Plans are extremely useful in making determinations about future property values, the information contained within these documents merely helps guide you to your own determination. You will still need to do additional research to discover the stages, statuses, maps, and other additional details about the undertakings. Consequently, when you speak to a potential buyer or make a decision to invest, you will be basing your informed prediction on an understanding of the community and the project. Buyers and investors will be impressed that you have analyzed a community's strategies, plans, and progress, and that you have made a determination about its future. They will be more likely to trust and listen to you when you have real information.

Where To Find Them?

If a municipality has them, these documents are typically simple to locate. Google the town or city, or use the Google research secret mentioned in the 'Research' chapter. Search for "Economic Development Strategy," "Economic Development Plan," or "Master Plan." Look for the most recent documents. Many are annual, five-year, or 10-year plans, which are fine, as long as they are up-to-date and the most recent versions. For example, if a 10-year plan was published in 2007, but it is only 2015, the plan is still valid. It may actually contain projects that only began recently. The more recent the documents, the better. The less recent ones, especially expired ones, will require you to do more research elsewhere since active initiatives are less likely to be outlined in an older document. Only through additional research, which you will be conducting anyway, will you discover the municipality's initiatives, and you will learn to do this research through practicing the lessons outlined throughout the rest of this book.

If a municipality does have a plan or strategy, but it is 12 years old, that poses an issue. If there is not one at all, that is pretty revealing about the municipality itself and its future growth (at least with regard to coordinated municipal efforts). Would you run a business without a business plan? Your odds of business success are much higher with a plan. The same goes for a municipality. Planning, in municipalities and in life, is what leads to success. That being said, many municipalities will not have an Economic Development Strategy or Master Plan at all, but do not fret, since these documents are merely one tool to utilize for your property value predictions. This book will outline plenty of other resources and tools for you to use to find what you need for your predictions.

In general, to find even more information on each initiative, you will want to browse the municipal website, and search Google for news articles and other information. To learn more and confirm that the information you learned online is current, you will want to call the municipal department managing the project. Each municipality lists the phone numbers for each department on its website.

Example
Let's take a look at the Table of Contents for Amherst, Massachusetts' 2010 Master Plan. To find it, Google

Master Plan for Amherst, MA, then download the document.[1]

Here is the full Table of Contents:

Which areas stand out as most useful to you in this Table of Contents? Since you have just started reading this book, the list of topics may seem intimidating.

However, by the end of this book, you will be able to easily skim the document and its relevant sections for many secrets that affect property values.

Master Plans and Economic Development Strategies are long and complex documents. Although I would love to teach you exactly how to understand them, doing so is beyond the scope of this book. It would require several dense, technical chapters that no real estate professional would want to read. Additionally, each municipality's documents are written differently, so these chapters would need to be incredibly long, detailed, and complicated. Therefore, rather than teach you master them, I will teach what exactly to look for within them.

How To Present Them?

Advise your buyers and investors of the goals of the municipality and what is being undertaken to achieve those goals, as well as anticipated completion dates of the undertakings. Tell them exactly where the municipality is dedicating resources. Next you will want to explain how each of the activities generally increases property values. Again, you will learn what to look for in these documents and how to delve more deeply into them throughout the rest of this book.

6. Transit-Oriented Development

What Is It?

Public transit expansions, new transit stops, and new transit options to nearby cities are almost always good for community growth. This section, however, is about one specific type of transit initiative, which is one of my favorite economic development undertakings. It is called Transit-Oriented Development (TOD). TOD effectively injects a new energy into an area surrounding a public transit hub or station. It builds places to live, play, eat, work, and shop around the hub. It transforms a neighborhood into a center of life that people want to live in and stay around after returning from work.

Why Is It Important?

As a result of TOD and comprehensive TOD strategies, I have seen neighborhoods sprout fancy residential buildings, mixed-use developments (residential and commercial), enhanced walkability, safety improvements, and much more. Property values generally increase in these areas, especially through thoughtful planning where TOD is coupled with pedestrian-oriented areas and mixed land uses. Examples of property value increases resulting from these initiatives can be seen throughout the country, from Arizona to California to Illinois to Maryland.[2]

How To Think About It?

Do any rapid rail transit or regional trains service the municipality? Does the local bus system stop at any of the same stops as the trains? Is there an associated parking lot for commuters? These are some of the factors that a municipality considers when deciding to create a TOD strategy for a transit hub. Is there a plan to create a strategy? Has a strategy already been implemented, or is there one currently in development? How comprehensive is the strategy? Does it include rezoning? Review it to learn if there are mixed land uses (residential or commercial), walkability considerations, streetscape enhancements, lighting additions, aesthetic improvements, and outdoor seating. If a municipality wants to convince people to move to the vicinity of the station and stay there after their commute from work, the strategy should be comprehensive and organized, which is the type of plan that will most likely raise property values.

Where To Find It?

Calling the municipality directly is the simplest way to discover TOD efforts. Additionally, the Planning or

Transportation Departments' pages on the municipal website, as well as the Master Plan or Economic Development Strategy, may field much information, including extremely useful maps.

Example

In a primarily single-family residential, suburban neighborhood in the southern part of San Jose, California is the Ohlone/Chynoweth Light Rail Station. Managed by the Santa Clara Valley Transportation Authority, the station is situated at the junction of two major freeways and sees over 60 trains per day. A comprehensive TOD strategy at this station resulted in significant new development, such as affordable housing developments with two buildings containing 135 and 194 units, as well as a 200-car parking lot, 4,400 square feet of retail space, and a 182-unit market rate apartment complex.

After the TOD-related construction began, property values increased by 7.3%, then continued to increase. After all construction was completed, housing prices within 1/8 of a mile of the TOD area were 18.5% higher than prices more than 1/8 of a mile away.[3]

How To Present It?

Advise your buyers and investors about the strategy, its timeline, the property's distance from the station, and the impact that TOD can have on property values.

7. Economic Development Organizations

What Are They?

Within nearly every suburb and city are municipal and nonprofit organizations that focus on economic development. These can be Business Improvement Districts (BID), Merchant Associations, Economic Development Agencies (EDA), Local Development Corporations (LDC), Regional and County Planning Associations, and Community Development Corporations (CDC) – which is a general term for any nonprofit organization that focuses on community development. Typically, each organization has a particular neighborhood or area of a municipality on which it focuses, and it delivers relevant services to that locale.

For your purposes, the organizations that generally have the greatest and most direct impact are BIDs and EDAs. However, depending on the size, activity, and nature of its projects, any CDC or organization can have a powerful impact on a neighborhood or municipality.

EDAs are offices within a municipal government. Occasionally, they are their own entities, but they are still always officially affiliated with the municipality. They are called by different titles depending on the town or city, such as Economic Development Departments, Economic Development Corporations (New York City, for example), Redevelopment Authorities (Boston, for example), or other similar titles. Regardless of the title, these entities function as the economic development department of a municipality; therefore, they conduct activities throughout the entire town or city. From job creation to waterfront revitalization to promotion of local businesses, their activities can run the full gamut of what is generally considered "economic development."

BIDs are legal entities that provide a host of services to an area within boundaries, usually in downtown commercial areas. BID services cater to the needs of their members, who are mostly local business and property owners within the BID boundaries. These services can include programming and events to attract shoppers, street cleaning crews, security, promotion of the district, advocating for the needs of their members, and other activities to revitalize, enhance, and grow the business district. Depending on the state, members may be legally required to pay yearly dues or taxes for BID operations. Although BIDs are focused on businesses, there are likely numerous condos within the district's boundaries, especially if the BID is located in an urban setting.

Why Are They Important?

Since BIDs, EDAs, and CDCs build communities, many of their efforts affect property values. From attracting new business to aesthetic improvements to crime reduction to housing developments, these entities can have a widespread impact on the area within their boundaries. EDAs, in particular, can have the largest impact because they can have the most funding as well as political support from the municipality for large-scale undertakings.

How To Think About Them?

Active EDAs are crucial, so follow them to see where they are undertaking projects. They may be involved in large-scale real estate development, redevelopment, and major revitalization projects. If this is the case, look into what these projects are and their locations. Are there adjacent or nearby properties? You may want to piggyback on the hard work of EDAs. They have already done their research, invested in development and planning, and pulled political favors. They expect big outcomes from this location, so jumping onto opportunities they create may be a wise idea.

If a BID does not exist, but one is in formation, how far along is it in the process? Formation is incredibly complex, and frequently fails. In New York City, BID formation takes about two years. If there are talks about creating one, keep an eye on its development. If one is in the final stages of formation, you may want to look further into it and research properties within its proposed boundaries. Additionally, you will want to consider the number of properties within the boundaries, the size of the buildings, and the size of the proposed BID's staff. A BID with ten staff members will be much more effective than one with a single, part-time staff member. Basically, the bigger the better. If a BID already exists, how long ago was it formed? If only recently, it may not yet have had time to impact the district. Therefore, it still may be wise to consider investing there, depending on the BID's goals, staff, and expectations.

Where To Find Them?

Regarding EDAs, look on the municipality's website for a link to the EDA website, which could simply be a section of the municipal website. The EDA website or page should include its previous undertakings and its plans for the future.

Browse the municipality's webpage for a list of active and relevant local entities by using the Google search secret mentioned in the "Research" chapter. If the organizations are not listed on the municipal website, Google the municipality's name along with the phrase "development corporation," "community development corporation," or other terms mentioned in this chapter. Skim the search results for relevant organizations, then browse their sites to learn more information and discover their activities.

To discover *current* BIDs, Google your target municipality's name and the phrase "Business Improvement District." Browse their websites and call them to learn more about their current and anticipated activities. To discover the *formation* of a BID, the best and easiest option is to call the municipality, since they will be involved. There may be many municipal departments involved, but you may want to first try calling the local Economic Development Agency. The municipality can also share its most recent status update or give you the phone number of the BID formation team and provide you with a list of active CDCs.

Examples

Economic Development Agency (EDA)

The New York City Economic Development Corporation (NYCEDC) is the non-profit, quasi-public economic development branch of New York City. It is involved in countless major developments throughout all five of the city's boroughs. To usher in the revitalization of Coney Island, the NYCEDC, with support from former Mayor Michael Bloomberg, took an instrumental role in the 2009 land rezoning of Coney Island. With this rezoning and redevelopment in mind, one of the most famous real estate firms in New York City, Thor Equities, purchased much of the available property in the amusement district. Thor Equities and the NYCEDC anticipated significant developments that will ultimately restore Coney Island to its former glory.

Although Hurricane Sandy set the amusement district back a few years, it is beginning to return, thanks to the efforts of the NYCEDC and The Alliance for Coney Island – a local CDC. The amusement parks are doing well: over three million people visit the district each year, a major entertainment complex is in development, a restaurant franchise recently opened a new site, and in the fall of 2015, the city announced it was both invoking eminent domain to reclaim blighted, vacant lots and investing more funds into the residential area. Although there are not currently any homes in the amusement district, the district's growth has already begun to spread to a residential area. There are already plans for new upscale residential projects, including a 40-story, mixed-use, residential/commercial building.[4] These changes signify the evolving face of the neighborhood and are undoubtedly the start of a trend that will send residential property values sky high.

Business Improvement District (BID)
The Downtown Boston BID did what most Boston residents had long believed to be impossible: revitalize the neighborhood. For years, the district had been downtrodden: full of vacant storefronts, and lacking much

activity. In a few short years, through its leadership in cleaning, programming, establishing a winter pop-up market, building relationships with developers, collaborating with the police, and spearheading other initiatives, the BID has rejuvenated the district. People finally want to live there; therefore, property values have increased tremendously. From 2013 to 2014 alone, the average selling price of a condo in Downtown Boston increased 16%, to $830,000.[5,6]

How To Present Them?

You will want to speak to your buyers and investors about the undertakings of local EDAs and other community development organizations. Outline their developments and how they may impact adjacent and nearby property values. Also discuss current BIDs, the potential for one, and how BIDs can impact values. Make sure to explain to them that the value of a home in this location will benefit from the hard work of the EDA, BID, or CDC, as this may ultimately raise the value of the residential property.

8. Grants and Funds

What Are They?
Municipalities and CDCs often receive grants and other funds from state and federal governments as well as other organizations. These financial awards do not need to be repaid, and can range from hundreds of dollars to tens of millions of dollars. Generally earmarked for certain projects, these funds can be used for upgrading infrastructure, developing land or buildings, creating websites, hiring staff, and countless other endeavors.

Why Are They Important?
When the government or other organization is giving away money, especially funds relevant to economic development, it may lead to a project that impacts property values. Economic development grants and funds are essentially monies from big government given to smaller governments or CDCs to revitalize, grow, or repair an area. For example, the State of California could decide to award $3 million to the City of Long Beach, which may use those funds to revitalize its

downtown neighborhood. The City might specifically utilize these funds to add street lighting, repair pavement, run a storefront façade redevelopment program, repair sidewalks, clean up vacant lots, remove graffiti, and plant trees. Together, these activities could have a big impact on values by helping to encourage shopping, reduce crime, attract homeowners, beautify the area, and increase the appeal of vacant lots to developers.

Wouldn't you want to know about these funds before other real estate professionals and homebuyers discover them? As an agent, imagine telling a buyer that "now is the time to buy because property values will probably surge as a result a State-funded $3 million revitalization project." Will your buyer be impressed? Undoubtedly. As an investor or homebuyer, wouldn't you like an extra boost to your property value on the government's dime?

How To Think About Them?

The path that big dollars follow is the path that you want to follow. How much is the grant for? How much will be awarded? The bigger the better. Small projects may not impact the municipality or neighborhood much. A grant for $500,000 could create a pretty hefty impact on property values, depending on the type of project. For that matter, even a $30,000 grant, depending on the project, could have an impact. Additionally, many times these grants fund only a portion of the project.

For example, a $25,000 grant could actually be part of a $250,000 project. Therefore, discovering this $25,000 grant will alert you to a $250,000 project that may impact property values heavily.

It is not important whether the municipality or organization has already received the grant money because many grants function on a reimbursement-only basis, which means that only after the money is spent is it reimbursed. However, make sure there has been an official announcement from the grantor that the funds will be awarded.

What is the expected usage of the funds, and where in the municipality will they be used? This information is essential. Is the municipality or nonprofit using the money to redevelop a waterfront or transform a large vacant lot into a park? If so, those may be worthwhile investments for you. However, is the plan to use the funds to study the migratory pattern of birds at the local pond, create a webpage, or redo the façade of city hall? Those grants may not be so beneficial to you. Using the topics outlined throughout this book will give you the understanding of what will impact property values, and how close in proximity a property should be to the project in order to benefit.

A final consideration is whether the municipality or nonprofit has begun to implement the initiative or project yet. What is the timeline and the status? If the project is already completed, it is probably too late to invest. Look for projects in the planning stages, or – if property values have not already increased – those in early construction stages.

Where To Find Them?

The easiest and most accurate way to discover whether grants or funds have been awarded to a municipality is by calling the municipality directly. Not only can they quickly tell you which grants they have received or will receive, but they can also share statuses, timelines, and explanations regarding where and how the funds will be used.

If you are not comfortable calling the municipality (which is always your best option), then browse the Economic Development Strategy or Master Plan since those documents may mention grants and how they will be used. Look for Community Development Block Grants (CDBG) and other large grants. You may also want to use the Google search secret for a municipality's website by using the terms "grants," "Request for Proposals (RFP)," "Block Grant," and other mentions of funds. Also, search the site for press releases about new grants because municipalities love to publicize these awards. If you find an RFP, what is the municipality looking for? Architects, engineers, or developers? Will any of these projects for which they are seeking contractors/consultants affect property values? If so, where will those projects occur? Perhaps those are neighbor-hoods you may to consider for further research.

You will also want to search Google for grants awarded to local nonprofits and other organizations. For example, let's say you are trying to sell property or invest in Staten Island, New York. You will want to Google "economic development grant awarded to Staten Island 2014." When I typed that phrase in, here are the grants that I discovered on the first page of Google:

- $6 million from the New York Regional Economic Development Council (REDC) to Brooklyn Brewery to expand into Staten Island, which will help create 140 jobs by 2017.
- $1.55 million from the New York Regional Economic Development Council (REDC) to help develop a giant Ferris wheel to attract tourists to Staten Island.
- $425,000 from the New York City Economic Development Corporation (NYCEDC) awarded to businesses to fill vacant storefronts in Downtown Staten Island.

If you were actually considering Staten Island, these three grants might all be interesting to you since they all could impact property values. Your next step would be to conduct further research into each grant to discover more details.

Example

In December 2014, the Trust for Public Land and Friends of QueensWay in Queens, New York was awarded a grant for $443,750 from the State of New York. These funds were earmarked for phase two of the organization's major project, which is to "transform a blighted, 3.5 mile stretch of abandoned railway in Central Queens into a family-friendly linear park and cultural greenway."[7] What do you think will ultimately happen to the value of properties adjacent to this park? I anticipate that nearby homes will become nearly unaffordable after the project is complete. Imagine telling a prospective buyer in Queens about this project. Wouldn't you expect they might be a little more interested with this new knowledge about the neighborhood?

How To Present Them?

Advise your buyers and investors about funds that will be coming to the municipality or local CDC. Inform them of the intended usage, where the projects or initiatives will be, and how you expect property values to be impacted.

9. Federal Housing Programs

What Are They?

Certain federal housing programs offer developers financial incentives for development. This is the case, specifically, when the program will construct, rehabilitate, or acquire apartments that will provide low-income tenants with housing at subsidized rates. For our purposes, two of the most important such initiatives are Section 202 and Low Income Housing Tax Credit programs.

Section 202

Section 202 is a program that tries to increase the supply of housing for the elderly. Developed by nonprofits, the public homes are tailored to the needs of the elderly and often provide relevant support services. To spur these developments, the U.S. Department of Housing and Urban Development (HUD) provides capital advances. If the project serves very low income elderly persons for 40 years, these capital advances do not have to be repaid. HUD also provides rental assistance funds to cover the difference between project costs and tenants' rent.[8]

The Low Income Housing Tax Credit
The Low Income Housing Tax Credit (LIHTC) is a program for the general low-income population. It provides tax incentives to private sector investors to fund housing for the low-income population, and investors claim tax credits, among other tax benefits, annually for ten years.[9]

Why Are They Important?
Typically, LIHTC in distressed urban and distressed suburban areas as well as small Section 202 housing in distressed urban areas generally increase nearby property values within a radius of about half a mile. The smaller the Section 202 development, the larger the impact. In one study, a few beds had the largest positive impact, and over 220 beds began to have a negative impact.[10,11]

How To Think About Them?
Rather than looking for current Section 202 and LIHTC housing structures, you will want to know where these developments are planned. If you know, for example, that an LIHTC development is going to be built in a

particular distressed neighborhood, you may want to look into nearby homes for sale.

Where To Find Them?

The way to learn about Section 202s and LIHTCs will be to pick up the phone and call the municipality. They can direct you to the appropriate municipal office that may be able to tell you where developments are planned. To find out which municipalities expect to have significant LIHTC development, call your state's Department of Housing by Googling your state's name and "Department of Housing." Additionally, using the Google search secret for the municipality's website and searching "LIHTC" or "Section 202" may helpful.

Examples

Section 202

In distressed areas of New York City, small public housing reserved for the elderly has had big positive impacts on property values. After construction completion, projects resulted in an 11.6% increase on values within a radius of 2,000 ft.[12]

LIHTC

A large-scale study reviewed over 24,000 LIHTC projects throughout the United States. It concluded that in un-gentrified areas, every 100 additional LIHTC units resulted in an increase in median home prices by 14.9% within a 1km radius.[13]

How To Present Them?

When speaking to your buyers and investors, outline these programs, their benefits for nearby properties, and the proximity of the property they are considering to the property utilizing the federal program.

10. Homeowners Associations

What Are They?

A Homeowners Association (HOA) is an organization that creates and enforces rules for properties within specified boundaries. It also provides services, makes certain necessary repairs, advocates on the neighborhood's behalf, maintains common areas, and can create a sense of community. They can function as mini governments and collect dues to fund their operations, and can be contentious in regards to their rules, enforcement, and dedication to increasing property values. Those last five words of the previous sentence are key: "dedication to increasing property values."

Why Are They Important?

In general, Homeowners Associations not only increase property values of the homes within their boundaries, but of neighboring homes, as well. Smaller HOAs seem to have a more positive effect than larger ones (the average HOA in the study referenced was about 150 homes).[14]

How To Think About Them?

Are any HOAs in latter stages of formation? Property value premiums are at their highest immediately after formation of the HOA, so considering a property within proposed HOA boundaries just prior to official formation may be the time to consider investing. Additionally, since HOAs take quite some time to form, it may be best to purchase within the latter stages of formation to increase the odds that the HOA will actually come to fruition.

Where To Find Them?

You will want to call the municipality to find out if any HOAs are in formation, and then call the HOA itself to learn its status and anticipated timeline. Searching Google may also yield helpful results.

Example

One study observed nearly 600,000 home sales in 49 counties in Florida and concluded that homes within HOA boundaries sell for a premium of just under 5% compared to non-HOA homes. This percentage translated to a nearly $10,000 increase in property value per parcel. Prices were highest immediately after formation, then began to very slowly decline by less than half of one percent a year, although continuing to remain at a premium. Further, the study found that even homes immediately outside the HOA borders generally sold for a premium over more distant non-HOA properties.[15]

How To Present Them?

Advise your buyers and investors about the benefits of HOAs, the development timeline of the proposed HOA, and how the property value may be impacted upon formation of the HOA.

11. Infrastructure Investments

What Are They?

Municipalities must invest in their communities to ensure continued functionality and growth. Investments can include creating an economic development plan, repaving streets, or traffic light replacements, among innumerable other initiatives. One area that can have a major impact on property values in the long run is infrastructure. This chapter is dedicated to investments in specific types of infrastructure improvements, such as upgrading or increasing capacities of public sewers, water supply, electricity, and wastewater treatment infrastructures.

Why Are They Important?

If the municipality is preparing for, or is in the midst of, upgrading infrastructure capacity, it may be gearing up for community growth. It may recognize that to handle increased usage, reach a new neighborhood, and attract new developments, businesses, and home-builders, it will need to invest in an expansion of its infrastructure system. This major investment is your hint that the municipality may deserve your attention as one that is proactive and looking to spark growth, which can lead to property value increases.

How To Think About Them?

Why is the municipality upgrading its infrastructure? Is it to meet the current capacity demands of the community, replace worn-down pipes, or repair broken piping? Is it trying to poise itself to be ready for long-term future growth? For example, the municipality may be extending pipelines to a new neighborhood so developers can build there, or it may be increasing the capacity of the current infrastructure to support a hopeful new commercial center. Understanding the reason and goal of the infrastructure upgrade is essential.

After you have established the reason for the upgrade, you will want to know the timeline. How far along are the upgrades? Has the municipality begun planning or construction? Is construction almost complete? When is the expected completion date? If there is no official timeline and construction has not yet begun, then the infrastructure upgrades may never actually come to fruition.

Depending on the type of infrastructure and necessary upgrades, construction can cost millions of dollars. Has the municipality earmarked funds or secured monies to pay for these upgrades? Has it received federal, state, or other grants and funds to pay for them? Does it have the money itself to pay? In order to complete these upgrades, there must be funds to pay for them.

Future plans are also important. Is there any mention of future developments where the infrastructure upgrades are taking place? If so, you will want to keep an eye on those areas. Remember that infrastructure is a more long-term project because, after the upgrades, the area will still have to be developed.

Where To Find Them?

Calling the municipality will be the quickest and most accurate way to discover infrastructure projects. Alternatively, you may want to look through the Economic Development Strategy and Master Plan, municipal website, and search Google for news articles.

Example

Stoughton, Massachusetts, a town about twenty miles south of Boston, suffered economically for over twenty years due to a lack of potable water. With only five ground water wells supplying the town's Public Water System, the supply was unable to meet local needs. As a result, in 1983, Stoughton's Board of Selectman established a moratorium on new water connections, which helped preserve the limited water supply. However, 17 years later, in 2000, the Massachusetts Department of Environmental Protection (MassDEP) issued an Administrative Consent Order that forced Stoughton to locate a new source of drinking water. To comply, the Stoughton Board of Selectman decided to begin purchasing water from the Massachusetts Water Resources Authority and to invest $1.8 million in water supply infrastructure. The infrastructure project was ultimately completed in 2003, and the final outcome was that Stoughton had a new water main and enough water to comply with the Order.

The upgraded water supply did more than just satisfy the MassDEP. It fostered the growth of the community. It enabled new developments to sprout, including a 230,000 square foot IKEA, a 143,000 square foot Target, and a Kohls department store, among numerous other stores and restaurants. With regard to residential property values, from 2003, when the project was completed, to 2009, total assessed residential values in the town increased from $1.9 billion to $2.8 billion. In other words, including new developments during those six years, total residential property values increased by 147%.[16,17]

How To Present Them?
When speaking with your buyer or investor, advise them about planned infrastructure upgrades. Explain how these upgrades may impact the area and allow for new development that the municipality hopes will

spark community growth in the long run. Additionally, discuss potential relevant future developments in those areas, if the municipality has publicized their goals and expectations.

12. Commerce

What Is It?

Commerce is about stores. It is about the mix, size, and types of retail, service, and food industry businesses located within the community. This category is especially useful in urban areas and suburban downtowns, where dwellings and businesses are intermixed.

Why Is It Important?

When new businesses open, this tells you something about the neighborhood. Do you think that Starbucks, Nordstrom, Target, Planet Fitness, Stop and Shop, Vons, and Olive Garden all open new locations on a whim? Absolutely not. They hire experts to do major, intensive site analyses to predict whether the site will be profitable for them. These analytical researchers are called "location experts," and their entire job is focused on the analysis of the profitability of prospective locations for businesses.

Admittedly, location experts look at some different criteria and look from slightly different angles than you will need to consider, but what is good for them is typically good for you. Some of the factors they consider that are extremely applicable to you include: access to highways, parking availability, traffic congestion, infrastructure capacities, rents, demographics, employment statistics, public transit, aesthetics, local business mix, land and housing costs, crime level, education quality, community opposition to developments, and more. These factors all contribute, on a major level, to community growth and ultimately to property values.

Therefore, take advantage of big businesses and their expertise. Capitalize on their location experts' hard work and investment choices. They do the rigorous research and analysis, and you reap the benefits. Just as people invest in whatever Warren Buffett invests in, you may want to consider investing where major chains and businesses are investing.

How To Think About It?

What type of new businesses are opening? Chic restaurants, stylish clothing stores, specialty grocers, and fancy cafes? If so, you may want to look into that area, especially if the area is slightly distressed. If the area is already booming, it may be too late to invest. Property values may already have increased, and other investors and buyers have probably noticed this area already. Keep in mind that if bodegas, pawn shops, check cashing businesses, or liquor stores are popping up, you may want to stay away. Those types of businesses are not conducive to community growth.

If the municipality has its own marketing plan to attract new businesses, that also tells you that it is investing time and resources into fostering community growth. Although the plan may not ultimately attract any new businesses, it tells you the municipality is proactive and growth-oriented – two fantastic traits that you can share with your buyer or investor.

Where To Find It?

For businesses themselves, put on your walking shoes. Walk around the neighborhood you are considering. You will also need to call the municipality's office and ask them what new businesses have opened in the past couple of years, and what businesses are considering opening in the near future. Additionally, Google the neighborhood for news about new businesses and those considering sites there, and then call these businesses directly to gather more information.

Example

Although the historically quiet Brevard County in Florida has not seen much growth in recent decades, the past few years have witnessed an explosion spurred by new businesses. Major businesses and their location experts analyzed the community, its demographics, foot traffic, and potential economic growth, and agreed that the county had staggering potential.

In 2011, businesses began to open there. By 2013-2014, the county had attracted an H&M, Ultra Salon, and an Academy Sports & Outdoors Store, among other establishments, and momentum was in full force. Now, the county is home to Bass Pro Shops, Five Below, Outback Steakhouse, BJ's Restaurant and Brewhouse, Baer's Furniture, and a new Publix grocery store. Additionally, in September of 2015, a Fresh Market grocery store opened across the street from the Promenade Shoppes – a shopping plaza with a long history of vacancies. Soon after, a mattress store and a Chinese restaurant sprouted up in the plaza. Next to come to the county? Possibly a Costco, which also has begun inquiring about available locations.

Residential property value changes have reflected the new businesses opening in the county. From early 2010 to early 2013, before the momentum really began, the average sale price of a residential property increased by about an average of 3% per year. However, from early 2013 to early 2015, after the momentum took hold, values increased at an average of 12.5% per year – over quadruple the growth rate per year compared to the previous period. In other words, for the three-year period before the momentum began, values increased only 9% (total increase from $142,000 to $155,000), and for the two-year period after the momentum began, values increased 25% (total increase from $155,000 to $194,000).[18–25]

How To Present It?

Explain to your investors and buyers the concept of a "location expert," and that major businesses employ them. Advise them that experts at several different companies (mention the businesses' names) have decided that this municipality is a good investment or are considering investing there. Last, inform them that capitalizing on the expertise of these analysts is a simple way to increase the odds that their property values will ultimately increase.

13. Aesthetics

What Is It?

Aesthetics is about the beauty of a municipality or a specific neighborhood. When you visit there, what do you see? For example, are gutters clean or are they lined with trash? Are sidewalks smooth or are they uneven and broken? Is graffiti everywhere or are the walls spotless? If there are vacant lots, are they covered in overgrown weeds or are they clean and ready for development? If vacant storefronts plague the commercial district, are they boarded-up or are they well-kept and ready to be rented? You get the picture.

Why Is It Important?

Besides the obvious facts that people care about physical attractiveness and that it heavily impacts property values, this concept is important because you can use anticipated, major aesthetic initiatives to help predict a rise in adjacent property values. Planting trees,[26] filling vacant storefronts, and beautifying vacant lots will generally increase property values.

Comprehensive beautification measures and blight reduction are always good moves for a municipality. When areas are cleaner, more beautiful, and better maintained, potential homeowners imagine living there, entrepreneurs imagine opening stores there, shoppers imagine shopping there, and developers imagine building there.

How To Think About It?

What planned or current initiatives and projects are under way that will beautify a neighborhood in your target municipality? Does the municipality or a CDC recognize any aesthetic problem and have concrete plans for a resolution, and, if so, when will this resolution begin? Look at sites only in the particular area that is being beautified, since the effects of the beautification may only have an impact in that vicinity.

Trees are a great economic development tool. Besides beautifying areas, they reduce home energy consumption and provide environmental benefits. Does the municipality outline tree plantings in its Master Plan? Is there a standalone tree planting initiative, such as the MillionTreesNYC plan in New York City? Find out exactly where the trees will be planted because the nearby properties are the ones that will benefit.

How effective has the municipality's program been in filling vacant storefronts and lots? It is very difficult for a municipality to fill such locations, so I would not suggest considering an area with many vacancies based solely upon a municipality's plan to fill them. Once businesses begin to sign leases or begin building on those spots, then you may want to reconsider that area as one in which to invest.

Where To Find It?

Look through the municipality's Economic Development Strategy, Master Plan, and website for any initiatives and projects that will beautify or enhance an area. Local CDCs may also have plans to beautify commercial districts or even residential neighborhoods, so browse their websites, too. Additionally, calling the municipality directly will yield helpful information. If it is available, they may even send you the list of locations where they expect to plant trees.

Example

Based on a study of over 20,000 observed homes in Phoenix, Arizona, a few simple trees can increase values. A one-percent increment of tree coverage within a 200 meter radius was discovered to result in an increase in MWTP (Marginal Willingness to Pay) of $3,364 for a single home.[27]

How To Present It?

Advise your buyers and investors about anticipated aesthetic improvements and tree plantings, and explain how these projects may impact nearby property values.

14. Historic Preservation of Neighborhoods

What Is It?

In an effort to revitalize and enhance certain neighborhoods that have historic character, especially distressed ones, municipalities can designate a neighborhood as "historic." This Historic Preservation designation is more than a simple credential – it is a powerful economic development and cultural tool. It maintains the historic character and look through required preservation of properties and upkeep of facades, and ensures mutual cooperation among owners to maintain their properties. It can also provide various types of legal protections to historic properties.

Historic designation can also make a neighborhood eligible for certain federal tax incentives, grants, easements, and favorable building code alternatives that can help property owners. Additionally, depending on the level of designation (local, state, and/or national), the neighborhood can be added to various historical registries, such as the National Registry of Historic Places or the State Historic Preservation Office's list.

Why Is It Important?

Throughout the country, designation of a district as "historic" has been shown to increase residential property values within the district.[28-37] Studies generally conclude that property values increase in the range of 5% to 35%, with most increases somewhere in the middle. In one case, vacant residential land increased by a staggering 131%.[38] Additionally, in the vast majority of cases, properties in historic districts appreciate much more rapidly than the market as a whole.[39] Even homes within close proximity to historic district boundaries typically increase by a few percentage points relative to comparable homes farther away (more than about 500 feet),[40] with closer properties faring the best. One study of San Diego concluded there was a 3.8% increase within 250 feet and a 1.6% increase within 250-500 feet of boundaries.[41]

How To Think About It?

Is any municipality in your region trying to designate a district as "historic?" On what government level are they attempting to do so? If they are seeking designation, how far along are they in the process? Are they waiting for approval? Since it is a complicated, lengthy, and labor-intensive process that is not always approved, the time to consider an investment there would be nearest to the actual approval as possible, before property value gains are realized.

What are the boundaries of this Historic Preservation area, and are properties available for purchase there? Inexpensive property will likely be available since the area is probably a distressed neighborhood, which, again, may be the impetus for seeking the designation. Regarding property value increases, I would expect the highest to occur within the center of the district, so that the property will be surrounded by homes that have the same façade, property maintenance, and aesthetic requirements. If the property is located near the boundaries, nearby homes will have no such requirements, which may result in a slightly lower value increase.

Where To Find It?

To discover whether any historic districts are in the works and where the current ones are located, you will first want to call your State Historic Preservation Office[42] because municipalities usually register with state registries before the national registry. You will want to search the municipal Economic Development Strategies, Master Plans, and municipal website for any mention of "historic designation," and conduct research on Google. Calling the target municipality's office directly will be the simplest way to discover any historic preservation efforts.

Example

In 2003, the New York City Independent Budget Office (IBO) conducted a thorough study of property value changes in all five boroughs. The office looked at historical data from 1975-2002, examining over 350,000 residential parcels with one-, two-, or three-family homes. Over 4,000 of these homes were in historic districts. After controlling for property and neighborhood characteristics, the IBO concluded that the historic designation district premium was evident in each of the twenty-eight years examined, and the premium ranged a whopping 22.6% to 71.8% compared to non-designated districts.[43]

How To Present It?

Inform your buyers and investors about the major impacts that a Historic Preservation designation can have on properties. Next, inform them of the anticipated or recent designation of the neighborhood and how the property under consideration may increase in value.

15. Walkability

What Is It?

Walkability is a simple but slightly vague concept. Essentially, a "walkable" area is one that is easy to navigate, comfortable to maneuver, pedestrian-safe, aesthetically pleasing, and encourages shopping. Amenities such as stores, coffee shops, fitness centers, and restaurants are located nearby and are easy to walk to and see. An area that is not so walkable may include a complex sidewalk layout or difficult terrain, and may discourage window shopping, and/or lack seating.

Why Is It Important?

Walkability increases quality of life, and people want to spend time in places they enjoy. Therefore, if the neighborhood is walkable, then people of all socioeconomic backgrounds are more likely to visit often and spend more time and money there. They will shop at stores and eat at restaurants, which helps the businesses in the vicinity grow. They will also use the space as a meeting spot. Additionally, people in municipalities with higher walkability are generally healthier because they spend more time walking and less time in cars. Why do these impacts matter to you? Throughout the country, walkable areas do not only increase property values, but values in these areas continue to increase over time.[44-49]

How To Think About It?

Generally, walkability is a factor in urban areas, suburban downtowns, and town centers, so keep that in mind in your research. In those areas, are there concrete plans to improve walkability? Look for pedestrian safety improvements such as red light cameras, 'No Turn on Red' signs, pedestrian crossing countdown signals, bike paths to remove bikers from sidewalks, and improved disability access. Will there be comfort improvements such street furniture (benches and chairs), public restrooms, and covered walkways to protect walkers from the weather? Are there plans to repair damaged sidewalks, add new ones, improve their connectivity to each other, or integrate them with the stores or shopping plazas? The municipality may also be planning complementary "wayfinding" improvements, which is enhanced signage to make it easier to navigate through neighborhoods. This signage may include backlit street signs, large maps with business directories, interactive map displays, and any number of creative and colorful methods to enhance wayfinding.

Fixing one sidewalk, installing a couple of new traffic signs, or adding a bench will not make much difference in terms of property values or overall walkability. Combining these efforts under a thorough walkability initiative is what can impact property values and community growth. The most effective walkability strategy will be one that is comprehensive, creates new and improved pedestrian-oriented streetscapes and walks, and reduces the need for cars. The more transformative the walkability initiative, the better.

Where To Find It?

Look in the municipality's Economic Development Strategy and Master Plan, search the municipal website, and call the municipality to learn about walkability initiatives.

Example

In a study of 90,000 homes in 15 metropolitan areas in the United States, in states ranging from California to Texas to North Carolina, walkability was shown to make a big impact on home values. In 87% of the housing markets studied, walkability was associated with increased home values. Homes in areas with an above average Walk Score® (a rating of the accessibility of daily living activities, which is only *one* factor in walkability) were associated with premiums of $4,000 to $34,000 compared to homes with average levels of walkability. Even those homes with average walkability, however, showed an average value increase from $500 to $3,000 per property.[50]

How To Present It?

You will want to explain the concept of walkability and its impact on property values to your investors and buyers. Next, outline the municipality's plan to enhance walkability in the target neighborhood.

16. Higher Educational Institutions

What Are They?
Higher educational institutions include community colleges, four-year colleges, and universities.

Why Are They Important?
In addition to providing valuable education, universities and colleges benefit their respective local communities in various ways. They provide high quality jobs, increase quality of life, bring in culture, attract high-income earners, and revitalize and clean up neighborhoods. Therefore, higher education institutions can gentrify neighborhoods and entire municipalities, boosting property values.

How To Think About Them?
Within your municipality, are there any colleges and universities that have plans for expansion? Look to the neighborhoods surrounding them. Are the neighborhoods around them depressed, distressed, blighted, downtrodden, or simply in need of a facelift? Higher

educational institutions, with their huge endowments and budgets, love to expand, and can provide a property value boost when they do. Where do the universities or colleges plan to expand to? Are they buying up land, and if so, what developments are they planning?

Where To Find Them?

Which colleges or universities are located in your municipality? Visit their websites and search for their Strategic Growth Plans, Masters Plans, or similarly named documents. They will outline their plans and timelines for growth. Look at their development maps to learn where and what they plan to develop. You will then want to call the academic institution to discover the most current status and timeline of any relevant projects.

Example

Northeastern University in Boston has been growing rapidly in recent decades. In 2001, they even expanded into the historically distressed neighborhood of Roxbury, an area plagued by crime. Along Columbus Avenue, the university built two residence halls known as Davenport Commons. The Commons housed two groups: one comprised of 585 students and the other comprised of 75 families that represented a range of incomes. These families were allowed to purchase a condo or townhouse in the building at or below market value. Additionally, over 2000 square feet of commercial space was also created in these structures.[51]

This $51 million development by Northeastern, combined with more of their own and other collaborative efforts in the surrounding neighborhood, have been a major factor in the revitalization of this section of Roxbury. Property values in the neighborhood of Northeastern's developments have consequently increased.[52,53]

How To Present Them?
Speak to your buyers and investors about the power that colleges and universities have to revitalize and gentrify neighborhoods. Outline the expansion plans of the local institutions and explain how the property under consideration may be favorably impacted.

17. SAT Scores

What Are They?

American students who want to attend college take the SAT exam in their junior or senior year of high school. They then include these scores, which are out of 2400, with their applications to their desired colleges. Colleges then use these scores as a factor in making admission decisions.

Why Are They Important?

High quality high schools contribute to high property values. How do you gauge quality, though? Can quality really be gauged by graduation rates, average GPA, or college attendance rates? For our purposes, it does not matter. We are trying to *predict* community growth, not gauge the quality of the current school. Therefore, all you will really need to look at are SAT scores, which are generally correlated with property values.[54,55] Although the scores themselves are not necessarily accurate assessments of academic ability, the scores do indicate a good deal about a community. They can be a general gauge of average income, professional job status of residents, employment rates, crime, and other socioeconomic considerations.

To better clarify the correlation between socioeconomics and SAT scores, here is an example. SAT tutors help students raise their test scores. At $75 an hour, who can afford these tutors? Wealthier people – not those typically living in poorer areas. Therefore, one of the reasons wealthier communities generally have higher SAT scores than poorer communities is that they can afford this type of assistance. Their high schoolers are then generally more competitive applicants for prestigious universities, which are consequently filled with wealthy students. So, although SAT scores tell you nothing about the students themselves, they do give you an idea of the level of wealth in a municipality.

How To Think About Them?

What are the SAT score trends at the public high schools in your target municipality? These trends, specifically, can help predict future property values. Are SAT scores increasing? Property values may soon follow since, again, SAT scores are correlated with many socioeconomic statistics within the community.

On a deeper level, even within municipalities, certain public schools outperform others with regard to SAT scores. Therefore, which neighborhoods in the municipality are served by public schools with increasing scores? You may want to do a little more research into those specific neighborhoods.

Where To Find Them?

Your state government's website may have a list of SAT scores. There, you should be able to find scores for nearly every municipality and each public high school in the state, and when you do, you will want to compare the data from year to year. In Massachusetts, for example, the state Department of Education has a simple webpage that lists SAT scores from 2004 to the present.[56] If your state does not post scores, there are usually articles from regional newspapers posting lists of scores broken down by municipality, so you may need to do some quick searching on Google for this data.

Examples

In eight neighborhoods in five municipalities in New Jersey, a minor 10-point increase in SAT math scores was associated with a 2-3% increase in median home value Zestimates.[57, 58]

How To Present Them?

Advise your buyers and investors about the strength of SAT scores as an economic indicator for a community. Then discuss the score *trend* for the municipality or particular neighborhoods as well as the impact you expect it may have on property values.

18. Summary

Economic Development Strategies and Master Plans

Let's go back to the Amherst, Massachusetts' Master Plan example from the beginning of the book.

Once again, here is the full Table of Contents:

Supporting Document A – Existing Conditions and Trends Report
Supporting Document B – Ideas for the Future
Supporting Document C – Community Choices Public Meeting Results
Supporting Document D – Community Survey Results

Now you know exactly what to look for in the document. Keep an open mind when reviewing Economic Development Strategies and Master Plans. What do you think will lead to community growth? What will make people want to move there?

Is there more than one relevant economic development project going on in the same neighborhood? Look to combine economic development considerations. The more the better, especially when you or your buyers or investors are in it for the long run. Just like interest, the benefits of economic development compound.

What did you Learn?
I have taught you what Economic Development Strategies and Masters Plans are, and what to look for in them. I have also taught you several economic development secrets that mayors, town managers, city planners, and Ph.Ds in think tanks use to build and advise others how to build cities and towns. These concepts, the methods to research them, and the way to apply

them are tools you now have in your arsenal to make you a more competitive real estate agent, broker, investor, developer, or homebuyer.

More important than individual economic development concepts, I have tried to teach you a new way to think. About the future. Mayors and city planners do not think in terms of "what is," they think of terms of "what can be." Now you can think from their perspectives and use this new view to understand communities and real estate at a whole new level. It's time to up your game by thinking like a mayor.

Acronym List

BID	Business Improvement District
CDC	Community Development Corporation
EDA	Economic Development Agency
HOA	Homeowners Association
HUD	U.S. Department of Housing and Urban Development
IBO	New York City Independent Budget Office
LDC	Local Development Corporation
LIHTC	Low Income Housing Tax Credit
MassDEP	Massachusetts Department of Environmental Protection
MWTP	Marginal Willingness to Pay
NYCEDC	New York City Economic Development Corporation
REDC	New York Regional Economic Development Council
TOD	Transit-Oriented Development

References

1. http://ma-amherst3.civicplus.com/DocumentCenter/Home/ View/3092

2. Bartholomew, K., and R. Ewing. "Hedonic Price Effects of Pedestrian- and Transit-Oriented Development." *Journal of Planning Literature* 26.1 (2011): 18-34.

3. Mathur, Shishir, and Christopher Ferrell. "Measuring the Impact of Sub-urban Transit-oriented Developments on Single-family Home Values." *Transportation Research Part A: Policy and Practice* 47 (2013): 42-55.

4. Fedak, Nikolai. "Revealed: 532 Neptune Avenue, Coney Island's Future Tallest Building." *New York* YIMBY 10 Aug. 2015. <http://newyorkyimby.com/2015/08/revealed-532-neptune-avenue-coney-islands-future-tallest-building.html>

5. Cloutier, Catherine, and Matt Rocheleau. "Property Values Surge in Boston." *The Boston Globe.* The Boston Globe Media Partners, LLC., 20 May 2015, Metro sec. <https://www.bostonglobe.com/metro/2015/05/20/property-values-surge-boston/s4w7zrI55EX-JQznHKlKNXN/story.html>

6. Ross, Casey. "Boston Real Estate Assessments Eclipse $100 Billion for First Time." *The Boston Globe.* The Boston Globe Media Partners, LLC., 12 Dec. 2014, Business sec. <https://www.bostonglobe.com/business/2014/12/12/boston-real-estate-assessments-eclipse-billion-for-first-time/2ySIkD9WUF1wKYuhB-wkBZJ/story.html>

7. http://thequeensway.org/

8. "Section 202 Supportive Housing for the Elderly Program." HUD - Multifamily Housing - Program Description. Web. <http://por-

tal.hud.gov/hudportal/HUD?src=/program_offices/housing/
mfh/progdesc/eld202>.

9. Black, David. "Low-Income Housing Tax Credits: Affordable
Housing Investment Opportunities for Banks." Community
Developments Community Affairs Department. March (2014).
Office of the Comptroller of the Currency, Washington D.C.
<http://www.occ.gov/topics/community-affairs/publications/
insights/insights-low-income-housing-tax-credits.pdf>

10. Ellen, Ingrid Gould, Amy Ellen Schwartz, Ioan Voicu, and Michael H. Schill. "Does Federally Subsidized Rental Housing De-
press Neighborhood Property Values?" *Journal of Policy Analysis
and Management* 26.2 (2007): 257-80. Print.

11. Baum-Snow, Nathaniel, and Justin Marion. "The Effects of Low
Income Housing Tax Credit Developments on Neighborhoods."
Journal of Public Economics 93 (2009): 654-66. Print.

12. Ellen, Ingrid Gould, Amy Ellen Schwartz, Ioan Voicu, and Michael H. Schill. "Does Federally Subsidized Rental Housing De-
press Neighborhood Property Values?" *Journal of Policy Analysis
and Management* 26.2 (2007): 257-80. Print.

13. Baum-Snow, Nathaniel, and Justin Marion. "The Effects of Low
Income Housing Tax Credit Developments on Neighborhoods."
Journal of Public Economics 93 (2009): 654-66. Print.

14. Meltzer, Rachel, and Ron Cheung. "How Are Homeowners Associations Capitalized into Property Values?" *Regional Science
and Urban Economics* 46 (2014): 93-102. Print.

15. Ibid.

16. Commonwealth of Massachusetts, Department of Revenue,
Municipal Data and Financial Management, Databank Reports. <http://www.mass.gov/dor/local-officials/municipal-da-

ta-and-financial-management/data-bankreports/proper-
ty-tax-information.html>

17. Collins, Edward, J. McCormack Graduate School of Policy and
Global Studies. University of Massachusetts, Boston. Study on
Investment in Water and Wastewater Infrastructure and Economic Development. January 2014. <http://www.newtonma.gov/
civicax/filebank/documents/56417>

18. Sandy Shores FL Realtors, and Melbourne Real Estate. "Brevard County Market Report for February 2010." Active Rain.
20 Mar. 2010. Web. <http://activerain.com/blogsview/1556576/
brevard-county-market-report-for-february-2010>.

19. Kowarski, Ilana, Wayne T. Price, and Dave Berman. "Fresh
Market Part of New Retail Growth in Brevard." *Florida Today.* A Gannet Company, 13 Nov. 2015. Web. <http://
www.floridatoday.com/story/money/business/2015/09/16/
fresh-market-part-new-retail-growth-brevard/32491265/>.

20. Kowarski, Ilana. "Coming Soon: More Major Retailers in Brevard."
Florida Today. A Gannet Company, 10 Apr. 2015. Web. <http://
www.floridatoday.com/story/money/business/2015/04/10/
coming-soon-major-retailers-brevard/25538453/>.

21. Owners, Paul. "Quiet Counties Poised For A New Boom."
Sun Sentinel. 4 Apr. 2007. Web. <http://articles.sun-sentinel.
com/2007-04-04/business/0704030404_1_home-prices-indi-
an-river-palm-beach-county>.

22. Freeman, Bobby. "Brevard County Market Report."
SpaceCoastDaily.com. Maverick Multimedia, Inc., 26
Mar. 2015. Web. <http://spacecoastdaily.com/2015/03/
brevard-county-market-report-for-february-2015/>.

23. Berman, Dave, and Wayne T. Price. "Brevard Property Values Keep
Climbing." *Florida Today.* A Gannet Company, 17 May 2014. Web.

<http://www.floridatoday.com/story/news/local/2014/05/17/ brevard-property-values-keep-climbing/9233945/>.

24. "1st Bass Pro Shops in Brevard County Opens." *ClickOrlando.com.* Graham Media Group, 4 Dec. 2013. Web. <http://www.clickorlando.com/ news/1st-bass-pro-shops-in-brevard-county-opens/23293866>.

25. Price, Wayne T."Brevard Sales Tax Revenues Showing Comeback." *Florida Today.* A Gannet Company, 13 Dec. 2014. Web. <http://www.floridatoday.com/story/news/local/2014/12/12/ brevard-county-sales-tax-revenues-showing-comeback/20312243/>

26. Roy, Sudipto, Jason Byrne, and Catherine Pickering. "A Systematic Quantitative Review of Urban Tree Benefits, Costs, and Assessment Methods across Cities in Different Climatic Zones." *Urban Forestry & Urban Greening* 11 (2012): 351-63. Print.

27. Seo, Kihwan, Aaron Golub, and Michael Kuby. "Combined Impacts of Highways and Light Rail Transit on Residential Property Values: A Spatial Hedonic Price Model for Phoenix, Arizona." *Journal of Transport Geography* 41 (2014): 53-62. Print.

28. Leichenko, Robin, N. Edward Coulson, and David Listokin. "Historic Preservation and Residential Property Values: An Analysis of Texas Cities." *Urban Studies* 38.11 (2001): 1973-987. Web.

29. Coulson, N. Edward, and Michael L. Lahr. "Gracing the Land of Elvis and Beale Street: Historic Designation and Property Values in Memphis." *Real Estate Economics Real Estate Econ* 33.3 (2005): 487-507. Web.

30. Clark, David E., and William E. Herrin. "Historical Preservation Districts and Home Sale Prices: Evidence from the Sacramento Housing Market." *The Review of Regional Studies* 27.1 (1997). Web.

31. Ford, Deborah Ann. "The Effect of Historic District Designa-
    tion on Single-Family Home Prices." *Real Estate Economics* 17.3
    (1989): 353-62. Web.

32. Gilderbloom, John I., Matthew J. Hanka, and Joshua D. Ambro-
    sius. "Historic Preservation's Impact on Job Creation, Property
    Values, and Environmental Sustainability." *Journal of Urbanism:
    International Research on Placemaking and Urban Sustainability*
    2.2 (2009): 83-101. Web.

33. Athens-Clarke County Planning Department 1996 Economic
    Benefits of Historic Preservation in Georgia, A Study of Three
    Communities: Athens, Rome, and Tifton. Historic Preserva-
    tion Division of the Georgia Department of Natural Resources,
    Atlanta. <https://athensclarkecounty.com/DocumentCenter/
    Home/View/291>

34. Mason, Randall. *Economics and Historic Preservation: A Guide
    and Review of the Literature*. Publication. The Brookings Insti-
    tution Metropolitan Policy Program, Sept. 2005. Web. <https://
    pikehistoric.pbworks.com/f/Economics+and+Historic+Preser-
    vation.pdf>.

35. Zahirovic-Herbert, Velma, and Swarn Chatterjee. "Historic
    Preservation and Residential Property Values: Evidence from
    Quantile Regression." *Urban Studies* 49.2 (2012): 369-82. Print.

36. Narwold, Andrew, Jonathan Sandy, and Charles Tu. "Historic
    Designation and Residential Property Values." International
    Real Estate Review 11.1 (2008): 83-95. Web.

37. Coulson, N. E. and Leichenko, R. M. (2001) The internal and ex-
    ternal impact of historical designation on property values, Jour-
    nal of Real Estate Finance and Economics, 23(1), pp. 113–124.

38. Asabere, Paul K., and Forrest E. Huffman. "Historic Districts
    and Land Values." The Journal of Real Estate Research Spring

(1991). Web. <http://pages.jh.edu/jrer/papers/pdf/past/vol06n01/v06p001.pdf>

39. Rypkema, Donovan D. The (Economic) Value of National Register Listing. Rep. no. 1. Washington State Department of Archaeology and Historic Preservation, 2002. Web. <http://www.dahp.wa.gov/sites/default/files/EconomicValue_ofNR_Listing.pdf>.

40. Zahirovic-Herbert, Velma, and Swarn Chatterjee. "Historic Preservation and Residential Property Values: Evidence from Quantile Regression." Urban Studies 49.2 (2012): 369-82. Print.

41. Narwold, Andrew J. Estimating the Value of the Historical Designation Externality. Rep. Save Our Heritage Organisation, n.d. Web. <http://www.sohosandiego.org/resources/estimating_historic.pdf>.

42. http://www.nps.gov/nr/shpolist.htm - A list of relevant offices in each state

43. The Impact of Historic Districts of Residential Property Values. Rep. New York City Independent Budget Office, 2003. Web. <http://www.ibo.nyc.ny.us/iboreports/HistoricDistricts03.pdf>.

44. Gilderbloom, John I., William W. Riggs, and Wesley L. Meares. "Does Walkability Matter? An Examination of Walkability's Impact on Housing Values, Foreclosures and Crime." Cities 42 (2015): 13-24. Print.

45. Handy, Susan, James F. Sallis, Deanne Weber, Ed Maibach, and Marla Hollander. "Is Support for Traditionally Designed Communities Growing? Evidence From Two National Surveys." Journal of the American Planning Association 74.2 (2008): 209-21. Print.

46. Meares, Wesley Laurance. "The Walkable Dividend: The Impacts of Walkability on Housing and Socio-economic Composition in Louisville, Ky." Diss. U of Louisville, 2014. ThinkIR:

The University of Louisville's Institutional Repository, Aug. 2014. Web. <http://ir.library.louisville.edu/cgi/viewcontent. cgi?article=1956&context=etd>.

47. Pivo, Gary, and Jeffrey D. Fisher. "The Walkability Premium in Commercial Real Estate Investments." *Real Estate Economics* 39.2 (2011): 185-219. Print.

48. Cortright, Joe. *How Walkability Raises Home Values in U.S. Cities*. Rep. CEOs For Cities, Aug. 2009. Web. <http://www.reconnectingamerica.org/assets/Uploads/2009WalkingTheWalkCEOsforCities.pdf>.

49. Daio, Mi, and Joseph Ferreira. "Residential Property Values and the Built Environment." *Transportation Research Record* 2174 (2010): 136-47. Print.

50. Cortright, Joe. *How Walkability Raises Home Values in U.S. Cities*. Rep. CEOs For Cities, Aug. 2009. Web. <http://www.reconnectingamerica.org/assets/Uploads/2009WalkingTheWalkCEOsforCities.pdf>.

51. "Officials Opening of Housing Alternative Heralded by City, State Officials." *News from Northeastern: University Communications and Public Relations. Northeastern University*, 9 Sept. 2001. Web. <https://web.archive.org/web/20020421113225/http://www.nupr.neu.edu/09-01/davenport.html>.

52. http://app01.cityofboston.gov/ParcelViewer/?pid=0902000010

53. *Engines of Economic Growth: The Economic Impact of Boston's Eight Research Universities on the Metropolitan Boston Area*. Rep. Appleseed, 2003. Web. <http://news.harvard.edu/gazette/2003/03.13/photos/EconomicReport-full.pdf>.

54. Sedgley, Norman H., Nancy A. Williams, and Frederick W. Derrick. "The Effect of Educational Test Scores on House Prices in a

Model with Spatial Dependence." *Journal of Housing Economics* 17.2 (2008): 191-200. Print.

55. Kay, Andrew I., Robert B. Noland, and Stephanie Dipetrillo. "Residential Property Valuations near Transit Stations with Transit-oriented Development." *Journal of Transport Geography* 39 (2014): 131-40. Print.

56. http://profiles.doe.mass.edu/state_report/sat_perf.aspx

57. Kay, Andrew I., Robert B. Noland, and Stephanie Dipetrillo. "Residential Property Valuations near Transit Stations with Transit-oriented Development." *Journal of Transport Geography* 39 (2014): 131-40. Print.

58. The Zestimate® home value is Zillow's estimated market value for an individual home and is calculated for about 100 million homes nationwide. It is a starting point in determining a home's value and is not an official appraisal. The Zestimate is automatically computed three times per week based on millions of public and user-submitted data points. http://www.zillow.com/zestimate/

Notes

Notes

www.ingramcontent.com/pod-product-compliance
Lightning Source LLC
Chambersburg PA
CBHW060623210326
41520CB00010B/1451